NINETEEN MILLION

ELEPHANTS *and other Poems*

• • • *by* HELEN BEVINGTON

HOUGHTON MIFFLIN COMPANY BOSTON

The Riverside Press Cambridge

1950

The Riverside Press
CAMBRIDGE · MASSACHUSETTS
PRINTED IN THE U.S.A.

NINETEEN MILLION

ELEPHANTS *and other Poems*

for David

ACKNOWLEDGMENTS

Thanks are due to the *American Scholar* for permission to reprint "The American Scholar"; the *Association Magazine* ('48) for "Mr. White of Selborne"; the *Atlantic Monthly* for "Dr. Major and Dr. Minor," "The Gardener at Kew," "The Salamander"; the *Georgia Review* for "Bluebirds Are Threadbare," "The Fool Killer"; the *New Yorker* for "Dear Prue," "Here Was Mr. Pepys," "The Suitor of Christina Rossetti," "The Rectitude of Dr. Johnson," "Margaret Fuller in Chelsea," "The Wishing Well," "Flight to Williamsburg and the Eighteenth Century," "Academic Moon," "The Monkey Cage," "Lord Cornwallis and a Carolina Spring," "Return from Summer," "Cooling Card for August," "Holly," "August is the Mute Month," "Mrs. Parr's Perfume," "Two to a Kiss"; *New York Herald Tribune* for "The Silver Bird," "Beauty and the Jeep," "Masquerade"; the *Saturday Review of Literature* for "The Poet Gay," "Of Dorothy Wordsworth," "De Quincey Wept," and "Night Flight."

CONTENTS

PART ONE

Poet, take the poet Gay:
  Lighthearted, fat,
Beloved of Pope, beloved of Swift,
  So genial that
His way of humming at his rimes
  (Poet, take note)
Lent a sweet tunefulness, at times,
  To words he wrote.
Beguiler of the coffee house
  Was Gay, a wit,
"Life is a jest" his epitaph
  That never fit
Dark, clouded Swift. Poor Pope could say
  Nothing like Gay.

NINETEEN MILLION ELEPHANTS

"The elephant is reckoned the slowest breeder of all known
animals, and I have taken some pains to estimate its
probable minimum rate of increase . . . after a period
of from 740 to 750 years there would be nearly nineteen
million elephants alive descended from the first pair."

——Darwin, *Origin of Species*

Now on my mind, my bellyful of woes,
Nineteen million elephants repose —

19,000,000, dark and quadruped,
Abide this evening in my heart and head

Since I took Mr. Darwin from the shelf,
And found another way to scare myself.

What I was after was a cheerful line
About survival, 1859,

Some words I read once, of a world abloom
With species, man and elephant and legume,

Inspiring hope that Darwin might, with logic,
Still offer a few vistas biologic.

I reached the book down to console my mind
About survival (almost any kind),

And leafed it idly. — To my stricken glance,
Nineteen million living elephants,

Descending from a single, timorous pair,
Began to breed and burgeon everywhere,

And there I sat with pachyderms. Alive!
I like, of course, a talent to survive,

But this was genius (whether Darwin meant
The true or hypothetical event);

This was a mating, say, of King John's reign,
Blessed, by Victoria's — let me look again —

With nineteen *million* offspring. (So was he
Lost in the beauty of geometry.)

And this was dream. By now, posterity should
Spring natively in my own field and wood,

Common as bluets, shy as daffodils,
Loud in the summer night as whippoorwills —

Imperishable company, at leisure
To rock the land, to multiply at pleasure.

They should survive, and set the poles askew.
But, *like us,* Darwin said, they never do.

"She would have discovered wonders anywhere."

What in this place would please
Her? How can I tell,
Of the felicities,
What sky of mine would please
Her, what leaf excel?

How can I tell —
Small lizard in the sun
And the persimmon trees —
Of the discoveries,
Which one?

Which one?
Mockingbirds in the pine,
Profundities
Like the wild muscadine,
Mimosa — hers or mine?

Any of these.

DEAR PRUE

(From Her Obliged, Obedient Servant,
Richard Steele)

At noon he wrote her to remind
A lady to be lovingkind,
Alert, by afternoon, for him,
Expectant in the interim
Of evening, hopeful of the night.
He wrote at intervals, contrite,
Impassioned, when it would occur
To him, so languishing for her,
From Button's Coffee House, from town,
To set a protestation down.
The more convivial he grew
The oftener he sighed "Dear Prue,"
And in forlorn dispatches said
He pined to be with her abed,
Would fly, within a pint of wine —
Another and another line
Of desperation, words that were
Rhapsodic of return to her,
Enough to fill a modest tome.
Instead of simply going home,
R. Steele wrote literature. (Dear Prue,
I wonder which he meant to do.)

Sometimes he must have thought, "So this was I!"
Then turned another page to verify
The secret testimony. Live and well,
Hot, lusty, curious — here was Samuel.
Here was the look, the semblance, here his own
Amazed accounting, for himself alone,
Of everyday — begun, spent, so to bed —
And how he must have marveled as he read.

A man he saw of grievous failing, dual
In nature, at once cowardly and cruel,
Vexed with his lot, mean, greedy, discontent,
A faithless husband, seldom penitent,
Teased by ambition, fretted by desire,
Who walked with dark mischance (the Plague, the Fire)
And felt it mock him and his chattels, wife,
All he possessed and was. Lord, what a life!

And yet a fellow lucky to survive,
Cut for the stone, miraculously alive,
Aware of ecstasy on earth, aware
Of dancing monkeys at Bartholomew Fair,
A fine hog's harslet or a chine of beef —
A happy man, bedeviled too by grief,
But pleased by quiet candlelight to note
His darling lute, his wife's new petticoat,

The endless spectacle he loved so well
Of life, of London, and of Samuel:
Sam at the play, St. Olave's, or the Sun,
Sam kissing Nelly, Deb (or anyone),
Sam with the courtiers in King Charles's reign,
Cocking an eye at Lady Castlemaine —
A man he saw, and hardly looked with pride,
Yet felt, no doubt, resigned. And satisfied.

I

Dr. Johnson hated a pun.
Mrs. Browning made a poem of one:
"The Dead Pan."

Not too scrupulous or wise,
Oliver Goldsmith told white lies.
Oliver Goldsmith, born a poet,
Told a fib so you'd never know it;
Owned a lie and called it a feather
Tossed in the air. "No matter whether
It floats or finds a trustful head,
Nobody's hurt," Dr. Goldsmith said.

Dr. Johnson began to stir.
Dr. Johnson exploded, "Sir!"
User of truth as if on oath,
Samuel, honest enough for both,
Rolled in his chair, began to mutter.
Nobody knew what wrath he'd utter!
"Go," said he (but his voice was mellow),
"Molt your feathers" — to the silly fellow.

De Quincey wept
And went on reading.
Which way he stepped,
De Quincey wept.
Books, *books,* BOOKS kept
Insanely breeding.
De Quincey wept,
And went on reading.

MR. WHITE OF SELBORNE

"My little intelligence is confined to the narrow
sphere of my own observations at home."

Mr. White of Selborne, walking, walking,
Met the miraculous. It was there
Like the pink hepaticas in his garden,
Like the Hampshire swallows, everywhere.
Owls hooted at him in B flat, purely,
Nightingales sang, all at concert pitch.
Even the echoes were polysyllabic.
Mr. White measured an echo which
Shouted in Latin: *Monstrum horrendum,
Informe, ingens* — and said no more,
Meaning no insolence. Titmice loved him.
Squirrels left their hazelnuts by his door.
Mr. White noted the flora and fauna
Of a world tuned like a mellow chime
To the miraculous, waking its echoes,
Ten learnéd syllables at a time. —
Mr. White of Selborne, walking, walking,
Had but to listen. Punctually, then,
The cuckoo struck a D sharp at evening.
Two fierce, quick notes sang the willow wren.

II

Chekhov was never rich. Yet had he been,
He would have kept a harem of serene
Fat wives, all with their buttocks painted green.

THE GARDENER AT KEW

Vistas I love, and gardeners at Kew
Like Capability Brown, whom England knew
As builder of the "ha-ha," a small ditch
In place of a garden wall to spoil the view.

When each rapt visitor cried "ha-ha!" which
Meant simply he was so engrossed at Kew
In vistas, around 1752,
That happily he'd fallen flat in a ditch —

Capability Brown, aware that prospects please,
Saw in the ha-ha capabilities.

THE SUITOR OF CHRISTINA ROSSETTI

I hear that he was shy, a timorous suitor,
Affectionate by nature, man and boy,
But deep-abstracted, given to grave employments
Like turning the Gospels into Iroquois.

A little odd and philological
For love was Mr. Cayley, even prim
To act the rôle of mid-Victorian lover,
Though as such did Miss Rossetti fancy him.

At wooing he was mild, I think: his features
Look rather pinched for passion, forehead bare,
Too cerebral for world or flesh or devil
To have left a flickering impression there.

Yet it may be that love turned Cayley giddy,
Brazen at times, and bolstered by delight.
The evidence is small. His way with women
One dare not place in too intense a light.

Still, there it was, a fashionable evening party
Where, taken by Christina, ill at ease,
The poor man hid for hours behind the greenery,
Composing a few open pleasantries.

At last he hurried forth, in buckled armor,
And stayed two ladies, fashionably attired.
To each he bowed, a trifle wan but valiant.
"Are you interested in the Gulf Stream?" he inquired.

In the end, of course, Christina wed nobody,
But clung serenely to her spinsterhood.
It saddens me to own that his fine bravura
Never did Mr. Cayley any good.

III

Poor Lamb. A stammer when he spoke
Improved his gentle little joke,
Which had a point — but one that went
Best with an impediment.

THE RECTITUDE OF DR. JOHNSON

(Dr. Johnson believed that he might get drunk
on an apple.)

Dr. Johnson, drunk on an apple,
With moral scruple
Still would grapple.

Dr. Johnson, abstemious man,
Drunk on a Russet
Or Astrachan

Or Golden Pippin in the fall,
Would look teetotal
And ethical,

Would seek, on apple juice in Devon,
Sobriety
And hope of heaven.

Upright he would remain, sedate,
On King of the Pippins
Inebriate!

The one I cornered
Had an absent air
And Leibnitz in his pocket — surely one,
So clearly learnéd, with his thinning hair,
To label scholar, Mr. Emerson.
I sought him among speculative men
Whom you admonished to be brave and free,
Man Thinking. And, like any citizen,
He had a fairly thoughtful look to me.

I'd say he was bemused,
As yet distrait
By perils of a monumental kind
To plain and fancy thinking in our day,
A man who had serenity in mind
But noted wryly from his reading room
The irony of your immortal quip
On popguns (since affirmed the crack of doom),
And turned to Leibnitz for companionship.

He faced the question,
Mr. Emerson,
Which thoughts are more infallible and wise —
On books, or on catastrophe, if one
May choose his intellectual exercise.
I think he took philosophy, aware
Of stars and portents in the evening sky,
And made of life a scholarly affair,
Being as brave and free as you or I.

The learnéd countryman
By you devised
Was bolder — but imaginary — taught
It seems the scholar's province, well-advised
In the vast flexibilities of thought
To comprehend himself, the world, and me;
Equipped to save us, every year or so.
Our leaning toward disaster is, you see,
Brisk, as you found a century ago.

I met a native scholar
With a book,
Late version of the meditative man,
Having the build, the academic look.
If, Mr. Emerson, you were to scan
His features — seeking the heroic mind
And the prophetic vision (overdue) —
I can but wonder whether you would find
Man Thinking. Now and then, I wish I knew.

Of riming lads who wandered
    The avenues of trees,
Surely you had considered
    The risk, as one of these.

Lord, of that golden number
    None walked a Cambridge don!
Or did his mind encumber
    With scraps yours fed upon.

Wiser you went and graver,
    Deaf to the turtledove,
Yet harped your songs forever,
    As any man's, on love —

A theme, had you reflected?
    Calamitous to learn.
So far is the heart distracted
    From scholarly concern.

ALL THIS FOR A PIECE OF SPONGE CAKE

"Her idea of perfect happiness, Mrs. Moulton used to say, was sitting by an open fire with an author and a piece of sponge cake."
—Cleveland Amory, *The Proper Bostonians*

I might choose Friday, shortly after four,
During the chilly months. By, say, October,
The blood runs thin, one needs an open fire,
Authors are cold and plentiful and sober,

Poets abounding, even into May.
Think of the hours and words and happinesses
I might reserve before Memorial Day,
Having just poets in, or poetesses:

Frost and a piece of sponge cake, Auden soon,
Spender beside the hearth at winter's ending,
Eliot of an April afternoon,
Dorothy Parker and the spring descending;

Or the cool novelists at summer's close,
Marquand or Faulkner — let the queue be steady —
Maugham or Capote. (Speak to me in prose.)
I find the autumn deafening already.

Felicity and fire and Hemingway!
Ogden Nash, lyrical and warm and rosy!
(How many sponge cakes is this, by the way?)
And, as Mrs. Moulton used to say, how cosy.

23

IV

Of Mr. Thoreau: so odd and frank.
Found the *Leaves of Grass* a little rank,
But wondered, when it came to this,
Whose thoughts he blushed at. Walt's, or his?

THE SAD CASE OF
MRS. LETITIA PILKINGTON

(A moral tale of the eighteenth century)

Letitia and her mate Matthew, a mild parson,
Lived, the tale goes, in conjugality,
Till the day Mr. Pilkington ejected
The lady from his bed and board, and she —

Being instantly to Literature deflected —
Began her *Memoirs*. Soon the lovely fibber
Had sixteen dukes contributing to her upkeep,
Plus, it so happened, Mr. Colley Cibber.

But seventeen patrons merely spurred Mrs. Letitia
To livelier anecdote (by now quite shady),
Till Mr. Cibber's own *Memoirs* required him,
And the dukes wept at so inspired a lady.

Within three volumes she minutely crowded
Her mounting recollections. While no one
Can blame the author, who was purely literary
(Nor should reproach poor Mr. Pilkington) —

Yet into utter fluency had fallen
Mrs. Letitia, once a household dove.
But for belles-lettres, so she might have ended,
And but for Pilkington, perhaps? — And love.

Clearly, as his ardor hinted,
Dr. Johnson approved the hue.
But was she pale, or deeply tinted,
Azure or indigo a blue?
Was she a pedant? — Mrs. Thrale
Looked prismatic to a male,
Every bright facet of the prism
Shimmering though his witticism.

SAMUEL AND BEN

TWO Johnsons in the Abbey lie
That houses poets when they die.

The one is Ben. Who could not tell
The other, Dr. Samuel?

Beneath a dimly written stone,
"O rare Ben Johnson" lies alone,

His grave so narrow and so thin
I wonder how they got him in.

While near the Choir, where late and long
From morning prayer to evensong

Has mounted steadily the word
Of God — can he have overheard,

How supplicant a litany
For Samuel Johnson, LL.D. —

The Doctor lies, among a band
Of singers of his fatherland.

Yet, yet I envy among men
Neither Samuel nor Ben.

(The grave of Ben Jonson in Westminster Abbey
is marked by a small stone in the pavement of the
north aisle of the nave, inscribed "O rare Ben
Johnson.")

27

V

Anthony Trollope ignored the stars,
Galaxies, planets, Andromeda, Mars.
Once, calmly, beneath a sky lit all up,
"I do not care for the stars," said Trollope.

THE SALAMANDER

"I fell a-crying, while he, soothing me with his caresses, said, 'My dear child, I don't give you that blow for any fault you have committed, but that you may remember that the little lizard which you see in the fire is a salamander.'"

——*Memoirs of Benvenuto Cellini*

The boy Cellini saw a thing,
A salamander in the fire,
Bright flame the path, the covering,
Where it moved scatheless and entire.

A child will possibly forget
What he may ponder hard and well,
His mind by every sight beset,
Visible and invisible.

Even a lizard, spotted gold —
If by tomorrow there be none,
Tomorrow, when the hearth is cold
(Oh listen, my forgetful one) —

Even a miracle is less
And less the heart's concern. For fear
Of time and its own waywardness,
Cellini's father boxed his ear,

To deepen memory, inspire
The lesson. So he taught his son
The salamander and the fire.
(Be careful, my impetuous one!

A precedent is good to learn,
When redbirds in the holly tree,
When flaming cannas, quick to burn,
Look so miraculous to me.)

MR. FITZHERBERT

At least the words they left of Mr. Fitzherbert
Are final. Dr. Johnson had his say,
And who will quiz him now? Or ask Mrs. Piozzi?
And who recalls the gentleman, anyway?

Still I regret, in coming upon his likeness,
That they should leave two portraits of him — here
The one, and neatly canceling it, the other
Mr. Fitzherbert, late of Derbyshire.

The first is full-length, of a man of honor,
Estate, wealth, grace, felicity. Much is made
Between them of the perfect host, the great squire,
His genial ways, the courtesy he displayed,

And that the whole world liked him. This is unquestioned,
Since Dr. Johnson hardly praised beyond
A man's deserts. The tears of Mrs. Piozzi
Seem possibly a little overfond —

Unless before the other, shadowy portrait
She must have wept. Whatever there of pride
They drew so late, it was a Mr. Fitzherbert
No one had thought to fathom until he died,

But plainer then. His solitude was plainer,
Though everybody liked him. To the end,
Said Dr. Johnson, he had a great felicity;
But, "as I understand the word," no friend.

31

They may have been mistaken. Or this dark portrait
Is not now, finally, the one they meant,
Not Mr. Fitzherbert who hanged himself on Wednesday.
But something kinder, a little different.

A BOMB FOR JEREMY BENTHAM

(1940)

The teapot he named Dick
And Dapple was his stick.
He cherished pigs and mice,
A fact which will suffice
To hint, from all we hear,
He was a little queer.

They say he cherished men,
Their happiness, and then
Calmly assumed one could
Devise cures for their good,
Believing all men the same,
And happiness their aim.

He reckoned right and wrong
By felicity — lifelong —
And by such artless measure
As the quantity of pleasure.
For pain he had a plan,
Absurd old gentleman.

His final vanity,
Or mild insanity,
Preserved him, in a case,
A sprightly waxen face,
A habit snug upon
His quiet skeleton,

Dispenser of odd knowledge
At University College —
Where surely it was fitting
That Nazis, bent on hitting
A real objective, sent them
A bomb for Jeremy Bentham.

I can accept the world, the plan
Allotted to the race of man.

But Margaret Fuller's brag was worse.
She could accept the universe.

Carlyle said, "By Gad, she'd better!"
And so did everyone who met her.

I wish to stroll an hour in the Vauxhall Gardens,
With a tall gallant and summer in the air;
To be a Botticelli or a Fragonard lady,
Or Nicolette the fair.

I wish to be modest like My Uncle Toby,
Just as Aristides, mellow as Lamb,
Incomparable as the dark lady of the sonnets,
And not the way I am.

I wish to reason with Mmes. Récamier,
de Staël, du Deffand, de Sévigné, Rambouillet;
To hear M. de Montaigne saying, "Je ne
Fais rien sans gayeté."

I wish to make a fourth on Wordsworth's honeymoon,
With sister Dorothy (and, of course, the bride);
To sit beneath a bo or a plane tree, thinking,
At Buddha's, at Plato's, side;

To find the Fortunate Isles, the Forest of Arden,
Avalon, Wapping Old Stairs, Cloud Cuckoo Land;
To talk with Hazlitt on gusto, Keats on beauty,
Byron on passion (grand);

To walk the Via Media, in clean linen,
The greensward and the labyrinthine ways;
To say, like the fly that rode on Aesop's chariot,
"What a dust I raise!"

I wish to learn of marriage from Mrs. Micawber,
Love from the look on Helen's face in Hell,
From Eve our mother, and Héloïse — and surely
The Blessed Damozel;

To pursue, to be pursued, like mortal Endymion,
Like a daughter of the gods, or sister, or niece;
To possess both bread and the million-leaved mimosa,
And a deep dream of peace;

To ride a hippogriff to the moon and farther;
Escape Wird, Nemesis, Wrath, and Doom; survive
To the years of Shaw, dying only like Montaigne
Of having been alive.

PART TWO

NIGHT FLIGHT

Stars I could reasonably explain
At wing tip, in the hastening flight
Of constellation and of plane,
In the propinquity of night
And starlight, in the upward air.
I thought stars were appointed there,
And finding measureless their worth
As company to cross the sky,
Among them I forgot the earth.
This was a foolish lapse. But I
Before had little cause to know
The world illuminated so.
Then, suddenly, it lay beneath
Us, glittering, kindled into light,
A million points that took my breath,
A million patterned in the night
To lanes, ways, channels, circles, bars,
A city figured into stars;
Celestial, insubstantial town
That never lifted in the sun,
But flared beyond a wing tip — down —
Blazing a moment — passing — on —
Till there was darkness as before.
(And, darling, it was Baltimore.)

21 passengers, plus baby,
A routine flight, a routine storm,
Destination Atlanta (maybe).
The Silver Line, is it safe from harm,
Its losses few and luck ascendant?
Pray for the pilot beyond the door,
Trust in the captain, the flight attendant
(But, lady, smile a little more).
Storms are nothing, perhaps, a flurry
Of weather, a queerly antic plane
Rocketing, playful, gay (why worry?) —
But look, the whirligig grows! Again
Little buffeting winds, now crazy, squalling,
Gathering anger, gathering might,
Winds of tempest. They lift us, sprawling,
Prancing, sprawling, frisked like a kite!
25 souls, with the child, aboard her
And a reeling kite has she become,
No skybird now of the eagle order,
Not silver now but aluminum.
Oh stare into darkness, faster, faster
The wind, the rain — wait, wait for the drop,
For the rise, the fall, the rise — the disaster?
Wait for the crash at the whistle stop.
Fasten your seat belt! None abating?
Airlines want you snug and alive.
Stare at the man beside you, waiting,
Clenching his hands. Will he arrive
In Atlanta? When? Oh soon, soon (maybe)

6000 feet (down) through a routine storm,
You and the man, in time? And the baby? —
Then, Captain, tell them, advise, inform
Atlanta, make clear our fond intention
Of landing — *when?* — on a glistening strip.
Reserve the earth. Oh be sure to mention
Our return to earth. Say the end of the trip! —
Then wait, then wait in the black mist, tremor,
Pray, voyager, pray, for time is slow,
Aloft like a bird, like a kite, forever!
Pay your ticket and up you go.

THE SILVER BIRD

A silver bird flies over,
Slow-circuiting, rapt in air,
Beneficent to hover.
No other bird is there,
Silver and swift and free,
That lingers to look me over,
Solicitous of me.

Toward the sky, the windhover,
I, blinded with dazzle, stare
And lift my arms openly,
Preening to discover
That, pleased with me, it flies over
Dipping a silver wing,
And almost trying to sing.

FLIGHT TO WILLIAMSBURG
AND THE EIGHTEENTH CENTURY

There were thunderheads. The transition was not too easy,
As perhaps is always the way. It was no sure thing,
Casual as flight in the limitless sky, explicit,
But a matter of cloud and disquiet and threatening.
To be venturers in time was a turbulent venture
Of wind and darkening mist, enveloped in space
And the minute hand of time — slow, *slow* in circuit —
And the fear of never setting down in the place.
Yet we rode in air. The craft was a hunter, soaring,
Accoutred, if anything was, to veer to the past,
Set to a plotted course and improbable weather,
To the unknown, and the fear, and the overcast.
But I think I should hardly take the journey over
(Not with the closing in of cloud, everywhere
The risk and cloud), not the going or returning,
For all the mulberry trees and the pewter there.

The past was, of course, restored: a quaintly authentic
Colonial A.&P. and Rexall store,
Quiet old streets traversed by coaches, or taxi,
Gay Queen Anne ladies and sober tourists more
Humdrum in look. The past in color and spirit
Was one of eternal glitter and candlelight,
Copper and gleam, the beautiful fact of order

And seeming peace after the tumult of flight.
One might take it so — or might say it never existed,
Even the sassafras and the trumpet vine —
Cry not to have come, or never to have departed
A reasonable world, serener than yours or mine.
But I think I should not again try the difficult passage,
It being too far, beyond in the cloud and mists
Of remembered time, of yellow brocades and mimosa,
Porcelain figures, and dreams, and colonists.

FLIGHT ATTENDANT

A maiden
(On the New York-Miami flight)
Commonly attends us, moving there
Like Hebe among the passengers, face alight,
Cupbearing, kind. They had a man to spare
This run, to do the pretty chores and smile,
Tucking us in for landings, strewing cheer,
Toting a squalling baby up the aisle.

I liked him. I was charmed by the career
He made of passing gum, and took a stick
Flattered that Eastern Airlines gave me one.
People felt lucky, with him, to be sick,
With so composed a breast to lean upon
A mile above the earth, excelling in
Forbearance, solace. But there was a flaw,
One imperfection.

He was masculine,
As brawny a hostess as I ever saw.
I learned from asking how he'd come to fly,
In Italy (the late conflict). How he'd flown —
As gunner, say? — he didn't specify,
Shaping no word above the quiet drone
Of motors, such as pilot, bombardier.
I never heard of flight attendants there.

47

Ascent was hard. Like scaling a dark mountain,
We climbed the perilous altitudes of the sky,
Wind-driven, lost in billowing mist, upfolded
To nothingness. Ascent was far and I
Of no intrepid mind, not a summit fancier,
Bolder in valleys, had no lion heart
For Helicons or, soaring five miles the minute,
Even for heaven or its counterpart.

Yet, strapped into my seat, heroic, ascending
As if by valor, in upholstered ease,
Eating my dinner of wild rice and pheasant,
A soft white blanket tucked around my knees,
I rode to nowhere in the company
Of sixty casual venturers, through the blur,
As if to empyrean unreturning
Each held a ticket as a passenger.

Uncharted were these high slopes. There was nothing
To speculate on — the black eddying space,
The mist, the cloud being part of the excursion.
Then sunlight, dazzle, struck across my face.
Then we were there! — the very crest, the pinnacle,

Emerged to heaven, riders in the sun,
By Eastern Time, observed the man beside me,
Twenty-three minutes out of Washington.

So the heights were his and mine. We were attainers
Of blinding peaks of sky, the conquerors there,
And he talked to me about the rubber business
That took a man so far from home, by air —
10,000 feet up (loftier than Mount Olympus)
In a silver chariot touching firmament
On all four motors. — Then, returning slowly,
It would drop earthward, make the dark descent.

PART THREE

I came for Koussevitsky and the moon,
Beethoven vying with the Pleiades,
For the sweet lusty evening, the night air
Impassioned as it was with symphonies.
I came for listening, in love with stars
(Whole galaxies) and Mozart. Mingled, they
Made suitably spectacular in the night
Both Koussevitsky and the Milky Way. —
But I could not deny that Hawthorne, too,
The Puritan, an awkward guest, was there,
Of whose severer taste in rhapsody
I grew, although reluctantly, aware.
I saw with what disquiet, what dismay,
The Early Fathers soberly looked down
On rapture in Massachusetts, her bold sky
Indecorous, ignited. Let them frown,
I thought uneasily, and then remembered
A phrase of George Moore's, which reviewed our plight.
"It's all the fault," he said, "of that damned *Mayflower*."
I tell you, Koussevitsky, he was right.

Man down the road
Near Huckleberry Spring
Reminds me of Ulysses
(Not the wandering
Sailor, but spouse
To Penelope).
Joined to his abode
Is a live oak tree,
A sixty-foot oak
For anchorage.
Man down the road
Loves foliage
And roots, I suppose,
The stability.
Ulysses loved a mooring
And Penelope,
And made fast his dwelling
And his marriage bed,
A tree for a bedpost,
Looking ahead
To everlastingness. —
But, oak or olive tree,
A man ought to sleep well.
Dreamlessly.

ACADEMIC MOON

I have been walking under the sky in the moonlight
With a professor. And am pleased to say
The moon was luminous and high and profitable.
Moonlit was the professor. Clear as day.

He had read, of late, how extraordinary moons are
Upside down. Aloft in the night sky
One drifted upright, in the usual fashion.
But the professor, glad to verify

Hypothesis or truth, when he is able —
Even, it seems, to set the moon askew —
Proposed that we reverse our own perspective.
And, on the whole, it *was* a lovelier view

Of white circumference — smaller now, he fancied,
A tidier sphere. This last I could not tell
From so oblique an angle. I only remember
Enjoying the occasion very well.

Lovely lady, why do you ride,
So daintily clad, so neat, so fair,
Thus through town and countryside,
Scurrying here and bouncing there?
Beautiful, where is your pride
In your conveyance? A coach and four,
Cadillacs, too, are dignified.
But when this vehicle at my door
And you, so decorative inside,
With thud and quiver prepare to leap
Over the ditch, through mud, through mire,
Lady, I wistfully inquire,
Have you seen yourself in a jeep?

MASQUERADE

In Hallowe'en false face
Whiter than chalk,
A small hobgoblin
On the sidewalk
Diverts all the passing
Women and men,
In a stark white face
From the Five and Ten.
Even hurrying people
Recognize
What a whimsical thing
Is his disguise,
The impassive false face,
Whiter than chalk,
On a little black boy
On the sidewalk.

THIRD AVENUE EL

I had a dime
And life to spare,
So I took conveyance
To Chatham Square,
Up with the pigeons,
Rattling down
From the roofs of Harlem
To Chinatown —
Starting in squalor,
A candid view
Toning to drab
In a mile or two.

Manhattan is a saga
Diversely told:
Past the Sixties
Trimmed with gold,
The topless Forties
Spired to the sky,
Nearer to heaven
Than you or I,
I rode from want
Up to pride and power,
And was down again
In half an hour

On the Bowery,
Making a tour
Of the gimcrack places
Of the poor,
Staring into moments
Dark and mean.
More for a dime
I've hardly seen
On a roller coaster,
Up and down
From the roofs of Harlem
To Chinatown.

How happy are the bellicose.
I love opposers who oppose

Extremely and rebuke with ease
The certitudes, the verities,

Who sneer at Milton, who deplore
My trees for being sycamore.

I pale lest each reproof may bring
To twig and leaf a withering,

Lest ill to poetry be wrought
By a fierce word, a chiding thought —

With like solicitude, God knows,
And kindly for the bellicose,

Lest they, disheartened, be made mute
By sycamore too resolute,

By Milton rising from the past
Whole, unrepentant to the last.

But none is visibly upset
So far, and nothing is ravaged yet.

Oddly, in neither quarter are
Any hurt feelings. Or a scar.

THE WORD IMAGINATION

I speak it out, the word *imagination*,
But with misgivings, lest the shape be dim,
Random for thought, a word upon the tongue.
I say the only one I know for him,

And with bent heads they write *imagination*,
Poising their pens serenely, having heard
Before these bright abstractions in the classroom.
They have no trouble mastering the word.

— *Imagine, then, a sparrow at his window,*
And a poet watching, lost, bemused so long
He is the fledgling, picking about the gravel,
Trying, perhaps, a little sparrow song. —

Agreeably they listen. In the notebooks
Now follows the pretty item, told anew:
A. *John Keats was a Romantic poet.*
B. *He became a bird. Aged 22.*

Twilight is in my lady's voice,
Quiet as dusk and drenched with heavy dew,
She who, in speaking, exercises choice.
Address to babies is a little mew.

I hear at times lute, cello, trumpet, reed,
Grace notes and pizzicati and loud purrs.
My favorite is The Venerable Bede,
A very lofty syllable of hers.

She can sound cold, hot, tepid, or gregarious.
I wish to God I were so various.

"It reeks," I cried, "of purple sin!"
But Molly murmured, "Or of sloes,
Or of the blackthorn, lovely in
The summer deep in plum." — This shows
A sentimental strain in Molly.
I like to think it tastes of folly.

I saw her spank the child,
A foolish, unruly baby
Ready to climb the bars
Too young, and tumble, maybe.
She looked exceedingly mild
And imperturbed by him
Until he ventured too far.
Then, hauling him down by the tail,
Without any interim
She walloped her roving male.
Over the buttocks, *whack,*
She trounced him, *whack,* on her knee,
Pleased, I think, with her knack,
A beautiful thing to see.
But, at length, believing him in
A dutiful frame of mind
From enough discipline,
She paused and turned him back,
And with a convulsive kind
Of movement to her breast
Gathered him in to rest.
So he was comforted
In a furious embrace,
Rocked, fondled, hugged, caressed,
Stared lovingly at in the face,
And warmed and quieted —
Till he gained momentum then
To start all over again.

BOY ON A RIDGEPOLE

I might weep for him. But fitter
Is a more reposeful air.
Pinnacles require a sitter,
Ultimately, and one is there

Straddle of the rooftop, taken
With his risk of life and limb,
And my heart is hardly shaken
At the spectacle of him,

Rider of a beam, a climber
Skyward where the vistas are
And the orbit is sublimer.
Clearly, once he goes this far

Into empyrean, with valor,
And with farther lengths to go,
Now unseemly is my pallor,
My solicitude, my woe.

TO SUSAN AT BIRTH

One gender to walk the wide world in
Is the feminine,
A plight that — softly to a friend —
I can recommend.

Little black hound of morning,
Having accosted the dawn
By eating the morning paper
And spewing it over the lawn,
Having chased an early fancy
And stirred her corpuscles up,
Baying the while to urge me
To be risen like my pup,
Returns to bed exhausted.
After raising hell around,
She sleeps, my complacent lady.
She sleeps, the little hound.

A LITERARY CAT

(Not you,
My draggletail disaster),
Hodge was a cat
Worth looking at.
Dr. Sam. Johnson
Was his master.
Boswell
Immortalized him, too.
(Not *you*, sourpuss.
Hardly you.)

THE ADMIRABLE WEASEL

"A weasel has his points; is graceful, courageous"
————Heading of news item

By weasel words be not misled.
In virtue is he garlanded,

Courageous, graceful, and maligned —
A lion and antelope combined.

Observe his lovely limber neck,
Lean hungry looks that him bedeck,

Bloodthirsty eyes, and four squat legs.
I think the little beast sucks eggs,

So deft, so brave, that with each swallow
He leaves an egg intact. But hollow.

I mastered the louse from where I sat,
A Hessian fly, a Buffalo gnat,
A mite enlarged, a flea with eggs,
Trapdoor spider with hairy legs,
Springtail, horntail, whirligig, tick,
Scorpion, shipworm, and walking stick.
I turned to *waspish* but to grasp
The disjunct structure of a wasp.
"A word," I said, "is a foolish whim."
How dull to find a synonym!

THE LADY HAS A BOOK

The lady has a book,
Of vellum,
A bright jewel, rare and ante bellum,
Gold-topped, on medieval herbs.
Or nunneries? Or Latin verbs.

The lady has an Item, but —
Odd merchandise — unread,
Uncut,
In tissue paper. In a drawer.
And Heaven knows what it's *there* for.

EASTER MORNING

Nodding calla lilies, tall
Stately tulips, fleurs-de-lis,
Lovely as a carnival,
Offered up in piety,

They, the holy day adorning,
Him bedecked in Easter dress,
Floral on this Easter morning,
Bountiful in its excess,

Riotous as the lady's bonnet
Freshly blooming on her head,
Bright the tag $9.50 on it.
"Lord, we glorify," it said.

TO MARY SHELLEY

Content thee with a visionary rhyme,
With incantation, with a phantom song.
It was the skylark, Mary, was a throng
Of wingéd spirits, for a little time
The fabric of a sorcery.
But it was song.
Content thee with a visionary rhyme.

REFUGEE, 1944

So lately has he come, there lies
About his guarded tale surprise
That words are speakable, that he
May try them. Even openly.

And of the world where he has been,
His thought is cautious still, and thin,
Lest to his listeners it give
Precision to the narrative.

Yet is his meaning never blurred
By loss, the canceling of a word,
When to his listeners the place
Is too apparent in his face.

PART FOUR

LORD CORNWALLIS AND A
CAROLINA SPRING

Cardinals were singing in this wood
(And Greene was clamoring for his blood),

As Lord Cornwallis rode through the spring.
Green was the shimmer of everything,

Of mimosa leaf, of loblolly pine,
The tangled growth of the muscadine,

Of great dark magnolias where he rode,
Caught in an American episode,

Posting through April, on the run,
Hoping to get to Wilmington —

Mocked by the enemy Greene, by fate.
With spring and his honor to contemplate,

Lord Cornwallis rode softly by,
Greene in his thought and green in his eye.

Like Thoreau, I hate the sound
Of my own footsteps.
He would travel
The grass, the woods, the leafy ground,
Unsettled by the grit of gravel,
Deserting pebbled roads for fear
Of any scuffle he might hear.

Infinities of goldenrod
And huckleberry
Kept him free
Of needless racket where he trod,
And, in the soft upholstery
Of moss, of pine straw, as he went
The quiet was magnificent.

And since the summer fields are wide
And carpeted
Where I have been,
Well-padded is the countryside
To make an expedition in,
I hate to walk this city street,
Accompanied always by my feet.

COOLING CARD FOR AUGUST

Think now of cool persimmon trees
And the gardens of the Hesperides,
Wet sandpipers by a wet sea,
Of imperturbability,
Fragonard ladies, and *vert-de-gris*.

Think now of green, of willow and jade,
Of a green thought in a green shade,
A life of sloth, and fronds of palm,
Of estimating the world with calm,
Any lyric, and any psalm.

Or think of hoarfrost, rime, dark, blight,
Of the eighteenth-century Mr. White
Of Selborne, brooding one summer's night,
Nipped to the bone; of his small, chill note.
"One little starveling wasp," he wrote.

Of the two landscapes — would you say authentic? —
This one I found last April. I had seen
Nothing on earth like apple trees so vernal,
And pink clouds flying. Lots of pink and green.

And grass! On Fifty-Second Street, it blinded
Like Cartier emeralds, so glittering
I winced and hurried in and bought the likeness
For the immoderate look it had of spring,

As one buys a green hat or pink azaleas
Or Casanova's *Memoirs*. — Here you see
The other landscape (just outside this morning)
With the same gaudy air, the radiancy,

Which, although real, is the old razzle dazzle
Of pink trees, green grass, clouds. It leaves subdued
My pretty daub hanging inside the window.
Otherwise, there is verisimilitude.

HOLLY

It being time, I look again for holly,
Now that the woods are gray and soft and bare,
Now that I move so readily through silver.
Only the evergreen has tarried there —
Of all the world this little green remaining,
Scrub pine and cedar left forgetfully
Beyond the summer leaf. It takes small cunning
In such a wood to find the holly tree
That in October needs more subtlety.

Topaz in the sun,
The last, the last,
The only shining one, the only
Laden tree, holds fast,
Keeps yellow in the mind
Immoderate there
While the slow-mounting hawk — the hunter —
Moves in air
To bring the grayness on.
I shall forget
The veering of the days,
And gold forget,
That there was ever leaf upon a tree.
(But not just yet.)

JUDAS SPREE

What can one say
Of a Judas tree all
Embroidered in red buds,
Paradisaical,
At a lunatic hour
In the December sun,
Electing to flower
Like a phenomenon
As the weather may strike it?
I like it.

Bluebirds were a cliché,
But I was content,
For their company, to give way
To sentiment.

Veering in air as they were —
Though I might digress
To hope that they would confer
On me happiness —

In the deepening sky they brought
Such onset of blue,
I would take the risk, I thought.
And proceeded to.

SIX WAYS
OF LOOKING AT A HUMMINGBIRD

(After reading Wallace Stevens's "Thirteen Ways
of Looking at a Blackbird")

I raised my head.
Whose Cadillac had I heard
Beyond the petunias?
"Oh, it's *you*," I said.

But would I mistake a Cadillac for a hummingbird?

★

Minuscule blur,
Gloriosa.
A lady after the mimosa.

★

Oiseau-mouche is the Frenchman's word.
Listen,
And say hummingbird.

★

Little father, sip, sip
Honey on the tongue.
But never give any
To the hungry young.

85

★

Looking thirteen ways at a blackbird,
You see a lack of the hummingbird's knack
Of flying in the air backward.

★

In the mouth of the crocodile
Of Santo Domingo
Feeds an intrepid bird,
Not the flamingo.
And, for all its far-vaunted intrepidity,
I've heard,
Not the hummingbird.

LOVE AMONG THE KATYDIDS

Katydids in the treetops
With *élan* and *brio*
Now fiddle their upperwings
To amour and deo,

An evening serenata
By members of the male sex,
Pleasing, I hope, to heaven
And the lady insects —

Whose silence in the moonlight
Is bleak enough to blight one
Provocatively sawing
His left wing on his right one.

AUGUST IS THE MUTE MONTH

(From a phrase in the *Journal* of Gilbert White)

August is the mute month,
In a doze,
Leaf-laden and lacklustre,
Comatose;

Green surfeited now, deep
In customary gold —
Wild mustard oversaid,
And marigold;

Now taciturn of thrush,
Of tanager,
Save for the drowsy word "cicada,"
Quieter.

THE MOUNTAIN IN LABOR

Clouds swirling threaten ill to planet.
Heavy, heavy as a pomegranate
Hangs the storm,
On us to fall,
Dark-bursting and diluvial!
Woe to us, woe,
More woe than weal,
Echoes in mighty thunderpeal,
Portent of cumuli
With spigots.
Soon we shall be afloat
Like frigates,
Awash like brigantines and yachts.
(I hide beneath my chimney pots.)

Then, like a timid opening flower,
It comes,
The little shirttail shower.

SIGN OF FALL IN THE CAROLINAS

September brings the golden sheaves,
Piled glistening in truck and cart,
The bright, flue-cured, gold-plated leaves
To the tobacco mart.

The full-length mirror in the garden
Is for a cardinal. I found
Him peering in my windows lately,
Baffled by his excess, spellbound
To find himself so much around.

Too many of the same a-kindle
Undid him. I went out to stare
Once, charitably, at my own reflection,
Hoping to note a vision there
As fearful to the mind and fair.

But in the windowpanes was nothing
Really unnerving, to mistake
For sunset or a conflagration.
I saw that I could only make
The bird amends, for beauty's sake.

Now on one miracle before him,
Bright-mirrored, is he free to fawn,
Smitten with self-regard (but justly),
While his mate lingers on the lawn.
And all his dithering is gone.

OCTOBER NIGHT

You know the way they come,
The moon and fog together
Over Christendom —
Equivocal kind of weather,
When oddly luminous
Is the night, and stars to spare
Dazzle down at us.
Yet everywhere, everywhere,
Landmist like a caprice,
Hovering and smothering,
Hides the earth in soft fleece
White as a heron's wing,
Till Aldebaran cannot tell
Where the lost valleys lie,
And I am invisible
To the moon in the sky —
Which to the silver platter
Above me, burnished clear,
Is no abiding matter.
But it does look queer.

THE RAINBOW

Some brag about a rainbow in the sky
Keeps racketing in my mind. One ought to know
How to discount these fancies, to decry
What any new Marco Polo says is so,
Looking him imperturbably in the eye.
But a traveler (he claimed to Idaho)
Told a disquieting thing, about a flight
Westward one morning in a shining mist;
Said he peered down, like God, from a great height
Upon a rainbow, red to amethyst,
Ribboned beneath him in the early light —
A band of hue no wider than his wrist.
And, he declared, this rainbow was not bent
To a bow merely; it had curved for him
Into a circle, girdling in extent,
Like the bright halos of the seraphim,
Like a small prism on a continent,
A crown on glittering mountains, rim to rim.—
So I am left, like the simple gulls of old,
To gape and worry over that pot of gold.

Looks well in green,
Bedecked a little extra,
A golden leaf,
A redbird
In the sun;

Essays to please
With every trill; is pleasing;
Is fair,
Is summer-favored yet,
Is one

Of melody
And blandishment,
An eyeful;
Provides a seasonable warmth,
An air

Of prima donna
Meant, I think,
To stir me;
Of competence to do so
Is aware.

SPRING PRUNING

I can lop a dead stanza,
Nip a line
To let in the sunshine
And moonshine.
But trim a mimosa?
Or a trumpet vine? —

THE FOOL KILLER

(There is a legend in North Carolina of
Jesse Holmes, the Fool Killer.)

When Jesse Holmes came among the people,
Lord Almighty! this is what he found,
Fools aplenty, swarming in the Piedmont.
"Fools," said Jesse as he looked around.

There they squatted, from the Appalachian
Down piney slopes to the coastal plain.
There they strutted in the Plateau region.
(High time Jesse was abroad again.)

Home from Georgia, a spell in Virginia,
A few dark dealings in Tennessee,
"Home," said Jesse, "in North Carolina,
Surely the Lord is expecting me.

"Hallelujah! Give me strength to scatter
These prodigal fools from out my path.
Amen!" he shouted and laid about him.
Jesse was mad, and they felt his wrath.

Like a scourge in the pestilent valleys,
Like a flail loosed in the market place,
Where a fool sprouted there came Jesse,
Mowing him down with a cheerful face.

Yet by evening, the greatest Fool Killer
Known in the South let his zeal subside.
They were too frequent in Carolina.
No man could smite each one if he tried.

Wiping his brow, Jesse dropped his mission,
Rocked in his porch chair, and took this view:
"One fool," said Jesse, "is like another,"
Noticing what he resembled, too.

PART FIVE

THE DOORWAY

"People do not invent; they remember."
——Yeats

I looked at visitors and grass
Alike then, with approving eye
Tight to the orange-colored glass;
At golden apple trees and sky,
Life and the gaudy passer-by.

And the one bright pane — in between
Dim somber violet, darkling blue —
Gave the contemporary scene
A glint and garishness of hue
That limited my outward view,

So that the hills, the shining meadow —
Impostures which the purple square
Kept to a bleaker tinge, to shadow,
To less delusory a glare —
I have remembered golden there.

THE VISIT

Even at the train, late as we were,
I begged to stay and clung to her.

She smoothed my hat, my new red coat,
She pinned to my dress a small white note,

And I held my doll with the yellow hair.
"Maybe," I whispered, "he won't be there."

My mother heard and touched my face.
But my mother left me in that place,

And I sat unmoving, waiting, still,
And the telephone poles leaned by, until

Hundreds and hundreds filled the sky.
I did not speak to strangers or cry

Or move or breathe. And the train slowed down,
Creeping into the stranger's town,

And beyond the window, there suddenly,
I saw my father, expecting me.

RETURN

Still there were the small gerunds
Taught by Miss Jane Harrower,
And the diminished hills,
And the streets narrower,

The old elms and participles
I had forsaken,
A time ago, for the
Exit taken,

And the quieter river
And trees less stately —
Just the fields of rhetoric
Ah, the same green lately.

MRS. PARR'S PERFUME

She had gilt chairs the shade of honey
And a golden, fragrant smell of money.

It was a perfume more intense
Than spikenard — of opulence,

Ease, fortune, and eau de cologne —
That pierced me to my marrowbone.

To wealth so heady, a nosegay
More odorous and sweet than May,

I gave my homage and, in hope,
Prepared to walk in heliotrope,

Musk rose and specie, gold and myrrh,
One day delectable like her.

NIGHTCAP AT AUNT LYDIA'S

My aunt Lydia took her nightcap like a lady,
Delicately and slow, a sip, a sigh.
I hovered near her, being nine and obedient.
I watched her from the corner of my eye.

Over her empty glass she gave the signal,
Two quick nods. Racing to the cupboard shelf,
"Which one?" I cried. She wavered and said, "Peppermint."
I should have chosen wintergreen myself.

My aunt Lydia poised aloft her little finger,
Then, while I held the bottle, stuck it in,
Dabbing her lips demurely, twice for corners,
Touching a dribble extra to her chin.

Each night I hoped for almond or vanilla,
But peppermint smelled best, Aunt Lydia said,
For all catastrophe. Then, swaying gently,
She locked the doors. And off we went to bed.

KISSING KIN

With kissing kin, Aunt Lydia urged the tie
Till she was deep in branches by and by,

Able to make her tribal revelations
Freely to the collateral relations.

They heard such tales of Uncle Samuel's daughter
As made the gathered cousins' noses water,

So that they sat about and sniffed for joy,
Blowing in concert over Katie's boy.

Aunt Lydia said what pleased the kissing kin
Was sin. They always liked collateral sin.

KISSING GAMES

When young, I never liked to play
Dominoes, checkers,
Lawn croquet,

Cribbage, parchesi, flinch, or lotto.
But I liked to kiss
Little Fred and Otto.

Only kissing games
Gave me a sense
Of skill and God's beneficence,

For I merely won at Rook or Pit.
Here I won Willie
When I was It.

We always rode in the undertaker's wagon
The two miles over to Westford. Manley said
That murdered people lay inside the caskets,
Dead gypsies with their throats slit — good and dead.
But I don't know. His grandfather laughed and took us
Saturdays to Westford through the fall,
And every time I yearned to be included,
If not too small. (Manley said I was too small.)
Then, bold with him, I rode in scorn of corpses,
Slid off the wagon, waded in the dust,
Lagged recklessly behind in a wayside poplar
Till the team was far ahead. (Manley said I must.)
I had to brag and lie and earn my passage —
In goldenrod and sumac pluck the flower
Safety, at all times, by a narrow margin,
Knowing thereby the glory and the power.
For the way to Westford was a terrible journey
Past giant poplars, danger, among the dead,
From which at last we might return, by noonday,
Till somebody else got murdered, Manley said.

THE PINK SHELF

I was entranced myself
With that particular shelf.
Each book of verse or story
Now banished there, I think
Had proved too amatory.
That is why they called it pink,
This roseate hidden lore
On a shelf behind a door.
And there I loved to tarry
With diligence sublime
As patron of the library,
Though a young one at the time.

Yet Miss Green seemed unaware
Of Ovid and Baudelaire
And me, with girls so shady
(Each pink seductive tome)
As *Manon* and *The Pretty Lady*.
I took *Water Babies* home,
For already I knew my taste
Inclined to books, either chaste
Or in Miss Green's collection
Of amours on that shelf —
But I admired her selection.
I fancied pink myself.

TWO TO A KISS

"There must always be two to a kiss."
——Robert Louis Stevenson in "Apology for Idlers"

No matter how
A kiss is put,
Three is a rabble
Underfoot.

Three is a throng,
Is hullabaloo.
The idea weakens
Beyond two.

Two is the digit,
Is company,
The *Ding an sich*,
Fait accompli.

TRIOLET FOR CLAVICHORD

Mistaken is all measurement
Save, lady, of the heart's maturing.
Forever of the lost event,
Mistaken is all measurement
To gage, by volume, passion spent;
By item, raptures unenduring.
Mistaken is all measurement,
Save, lady, of the heart's maturing.

YARDSTICK

Tall as an apple tree is taller,
Inch for inch from planet to sky,
Than ordinary. I thought I was smaller.
Yet backed to an apple tree, am I

Its five foot two, and a trifle broader
Than limb or trunk, without my shoes
High as a treetop — which were odder
If it were sycamore or spruce.

WORDS ARE ANYBODY'S

Words are anybody's
Equitable things,
Like *whortleberries* and *lapwings,*

Like *missel thrush,*
And *mackerel sky,*
Shenandoah and the river *Wye,*

Linnet and *love*
And *frangipane,*
All within the public domain.

No matter whose quince
Or juniper tree,
Anything I say belongs to me.

If this must be my hapless choice,
My recompense, let me rejoice
In mild parades of everyday,
And deck myself in mild array.

Let me serenely recognize
Beneath this masterly disguise,
My customary self arrayed,
Proper for the same parade.

JOURNAL INTIME

"On this day my Niece Brown was delivered of her 4th
child, a girl, which makes the 41st of my nephews and
nieces now living. Boiled up some apricots with sugar
to preserve them."
————Gilbert White, *Journal,* August 20, 1784

I must begin my Journal, say, mañana,
When I find diligence, serve God, and mend,
And sift my days and number my increases,
And the apricots are ripe at summer's end;

When I have learned, like Mr. White of Selborne,
The keep of small dominions, and I am
Like him fair-spoken: for July, the swallows,
Or, for December, "Here and there a lamb";

Meticulous to note, it being April,
The amorous finches (so is spring unfurled),
To cry the first hepatica and titmouse,
"A green woodpecker laughs at all the world";

And pleased to turn, like Mr. White reposeful,
With open mind to the advanced affairs
Of June: "Swifts sit hard," "Goose resorts to gander,"
"Ants, big with egg, come out from under the stairs."

It will be time to item my possessions
When they grow seasonable: for August, say,
The waxwings — or a plenitude of nieces;
When the apricots bear witness, it is May.

115